THE
AIKI-DO BOOK

AL *KYU*

FUN FOR
EVERYONE

WWW.AIKIDO.SCHOOL

Edition
Aikido School Ando

Concept and design
Edo Slui

Illustrations
Ferdy Remijn | ferdyremijn.nl

ISBN
978-1077-48-23-64

Thanks to
Wim en Anne Slui, Elan Geelen, Annemiek Engelen, dr. Monica Hriscu

INTRODUCTION OF THE SENSEI

Dear Aikidoka,

My name is Edo Slui and I made this book to inspire all
Aikidokas just like you! I had this plan already for a long, long
time but finally here it is. You are holding it right now. The Ando
Aiki-Do book. It's an addition to my other books
'Aikido sayings and proverbs' and **'Ik Marga'** . These books
are also nice to have on your bookshelf. Just like you I started
Aikido at a young age together with my sister Anne.
As Aikidoka at the age of 12 and 10 years, we never
thought we were going to be the youngest shodans in
the Netherlands. And that we were going to teach groups
in our own Dojo as students of Christian Tissier shihan we
could not have imagined. But here we are, having our own dojo
named Ando. A combination of our first names. Did you know
Ando means in Japanese 'peaceful way'?

Of course we could not have done this all without the support
of our parents Wim and Marga Slui. They helped us to reach a
lot of what we have been accomplishing right now.

Passionate and fascinated by Aikido, sadly our mother passed
away on the 14th of April 2012. Her ideas still live in our or-
ganization. We teach groups now on 4 different locations in
Eindhoven. Grand masters from all over the world join us every
year to share Aikido with everyone in our dojo. We both are cur-
rently 5th Dan Shidoin and our sensei is
Yoshimitsu Yamada shihan. He is one of the last students who
learned Aikido from the founder Morihei Ueshiba as Uchi Deshi.

Would you like to stay informed, or visit us in the Dojo in
Holland? Check our website: www.aikido.school or our
Facebook page.

THE DRESSING ROOM

▶ Do you know which door Joyce should open to find the right dressing room?

MIKA—JO

▶ Wesley dropped a number of Jos. Do you know which one is at the bottom of the stack? Circle this Jo.

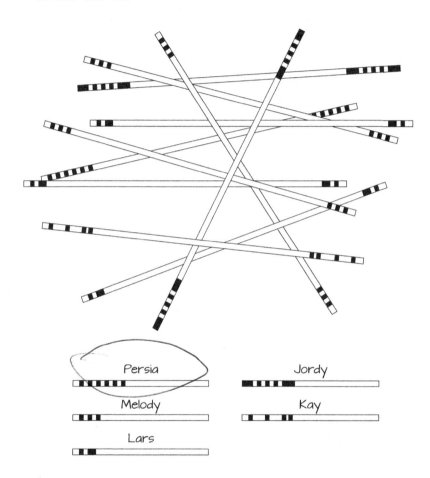

Persia

Jordy

Melody

Kay

Lars

You can play this game at the Dojo with real Jos!
(Do not forget to put your name on your Jo.)

ON MY WAY TO A SEMINAR

VERTICAL
1. Something for the break
2. Wooden sword
3. Something for thirst
5. Medical helper
8. Belt
9. Staff

HORIZONTAL
4. Wooden knife
6. Japanese clothing
7. Seminarbook
10. Dojo shoes

TANGLED UP OBI

▶ Do you know who's Obi is tangled up?
Follow the lines and find out.

Sam

Jeroen

Shanfanu

Stephan

WORDSEEKER

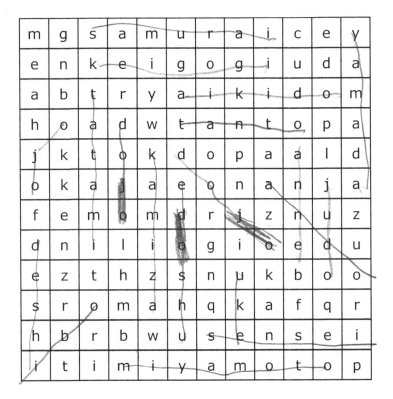

m	g	s	a	m	u	r	a	i	c	e	y
e	n	k	e	i	g	o	g	i	u	d	a
a	b	t	r	y	a	i	k	i	d	o	m
h	o	a	d	w	t	a	n	t	o	p	a
j	k	t	o	k	d	o	p	a	a	l	d
o	k	a	j	a	e	o	n	a	n	j	a
f	e	m	o	m	d	r	j	z	n	u	z
d	n	i	l	i	o	g	i	o	e	d	u
e	z	t	h	z	s	n	u	k	b	o	o
s	r	o	m	a	h	q	k	a	f	q	r
h	b	r	b	w	u	s	e	n	s	e	i
i	t	i	m	i	y	a	m	o	t	o	p

▶ Can you find all the hidden words?! Cross out the ones you already found.

Yamada	Obi	Ando	Sensei
Dojo	Kamiza	Tanto	Judo
Jo	Doshu	Anne	Miyamoto
Bokken	Uke	Tatami	Edo
Dojo	Anne	Keigogi	Deshi
Tori	Tatami	Samurai	Aikido

TRASH AROUND THE DOJO

Circle the trash around the Dojo. Check everything off the list and tell how long it takes before the waste is gone completely.

Cigarette 1. ✓
Banana peel 2. ✓
Coca Cola tin 3. ✓
Bottle of soda 4. ✓
Plastic bag 5. ✓
Chewing gum 6. ✓
Glass bottle 7. ✓

a. Million years
b. 5-10 years
c. 20-25 years
d. 10-25 years
e. 1-5 years
f. 4-6 weeks
g. 1,5 - 50 years

Answer: 1e 2f 3g 4b 5d 6c 7a

RANKING THE SENPAI

How well do you know each other? With this senpai game you will get to know yourself and the others much better. Write down on the chart who you think should be on top of the list. If you are finished, discuss the ranking.

- ★ who is the slowest in the dressing room?
- ★ who leaves his suit the longest in his or her bag?
- ★ who can not eat with chop sticks?
- ★ who is the fastest with his obi?
- ★ who is the champion nose picker?
- ★ who is the fart champion?
- ★ who is the best instructor?
- ★ who is the best helper with the tatami mats?
- ★ who is most of the time an example for the group?
- ★ who is doing the utmost in the training?
- ★ who is too social on the mat?
- ★ who is taking a shower after training?
- ★ who can sleep on the tatami?
- ★ who is the loudest snorer?

★ SENPAI RANKING ★

NO.1 ....

NO.2 ....

NO.3 ....

NO.4 ....

NO.5 ....

NO.6 ....

NO.7 ....

NO.8 ....

★ SENPAI RANKING ★

NO.1 ....

NO.2 ....

NO.3 ....

NO.4 ....

NO.5 ....

NO.6 ....

NO.7 ....

NO.8 ....

If you need more, copy this page or draw your own cards.

▶ At what time do you set the alarm?

At Ando the class is planned at 10 o'clock a.m. .

What needs to be done in the morning before you go? Get dressed, take a shower, have your breakfast, walk the dog, pack your bag, get changed and handover your passport.

Draw your answer in the clock.

AIKIDO SAYINGS AND PROVERBS

1 ALIVE AND MAE-GIRI
2 GET OFF ON THE WRONG HANMI
3 A KEIKO IS WORTH A THOUSAND WORDS
4 A FOOT IN THE DOJO
5 A TATAMI'S DISTANCE
6 A KEIKO A DAY KEEPS THE DOCTOR AWAY
7 PUSH THE TATAMI
8 IF THE ZORI FITS
9 PUT YOUR BEST ZORI FORWARD
10 A KATANA TO CUT A CAKE

▶ Do you know the meaning of these proverbs?

.... a To complete the first step in a process
.... b Definitely alive; lively and active
.... c Use disproportionate force to overcome a minor problem
.... d To attempt to extend the current limits of performance
.... e Embark on a journey or task with purpose and gusto
.... f A picture tells a story just as a large amount of text
.... g A good way to stay healthy
.... h A short distance
.... i If a description applies to you, then accept it
.... j Take a bad start to a project or relationship

1b, 2j, 3f, 4a, 5h, 6g, 7d, 8i, 9e, 10c

DRAW THE REFLECTION

▶ Do you know the name of this attack? Finish Eric's gi.

gyaku hannai

Katate dori

LEAVE ON TIME

The two sisters are getting dressed in 10 minutes and also help with the tatami mats. That will take them 15 minutes .The trip from home to the Dojo is 13 minutes.

▶ At what time do the sisters have to leave to be on time for the training? Set the alarm at the right time.

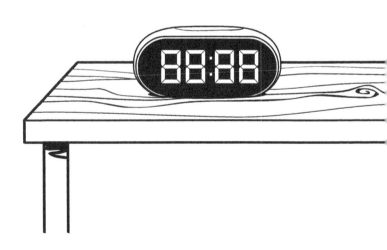

Answer: twenty two minutes over six she has to leave

CROSSWORD PUZZLE

▶ Do you know all these Japanese words?
You may use some help of the internet.

HORIZONTAL

2. Walking on the knees
3. Turn of the body
5. Founder's first name
8. Outside
11. Clothing on the tatami
13. Roll
14. Strike to the head
17. Art we practice

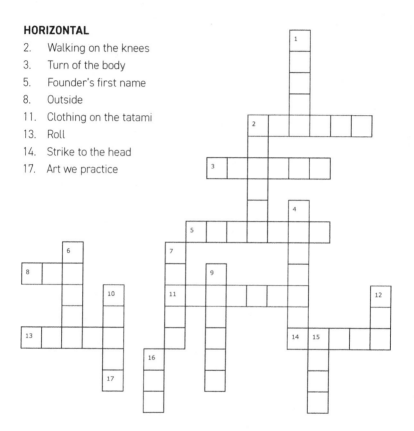

7. First technique

VERTICAL

1. Front step
2. Teacher
4. Founder's last name
6. Posture

9. Second technique
10. Sitting on the knees
12. Belt
15. Defender
16. Attacker

A CARD FOR SENSEI

▶ Can you, as a senpai, correct the text before your kohai will send this to sensei?

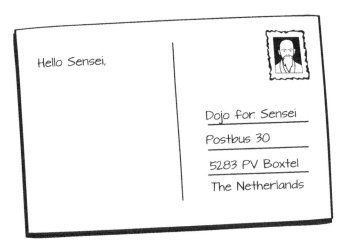

Hello Sensei,

Dojo for. Sensei

Postbus 30

5283 PV Boxtel

The Netherlands

Hello Sensei,

Last week we went to Barceloona for a seminar. The weather was great, very Sunny 24 degres so a nice temperature. We learned a lod from Michelle Feilen sensei. But time fliez when you are having vun. His training was very nice but hart. We practiced a lot of Kokyu nagee's and Yonkyo.
I have a lot of bruises and muscle ache. The aikidokas I met here are all verry friendly and we had a nice lunch together. Hope to see you soon, I can't waid to show you what I have learnet.

Greetz

Answer: there are at least 10 mistakes made

THE ZORI MAZE

QUICK LUNCH

Training is finished at noon and Peter is busy folding his hakama and wonders how much time he has for lunch. The next training starts at 2 o'clock p.m. It takes him 10 minutes to fold his hakama, 10 minutes to get changed and a 5 minute walk from the Dojo to the lunchroom. To change back into his gi and hakama will take another 15 minutes.

▶ How much time will Peter have for his lunch? Make sure he's back on the tatami before sensei is.

....

Answer: he has a lunch break of one hour and twentyfive minutes

MAKE YOUR OWN CHOCOLATE SPREAD

Originally chocopaste was made this way:

- 1/2 banana
- 1/2 avocado
- 1 spoon cocoa powder
- 1 teaspoon dry coconut
(If you like it, of course.)

Preparation

1. Mix the banana and the avocado till you have a smooth paste.

2. Add the cocoa and the coconut and mix it all together.

3. And now the most important thing, put it on a sandwich and taste it!!

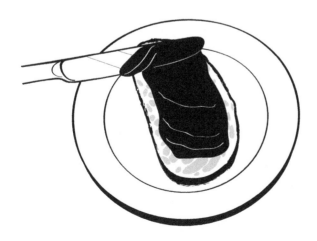

DRAW A POSTCARD FOR YOUR SENSEI

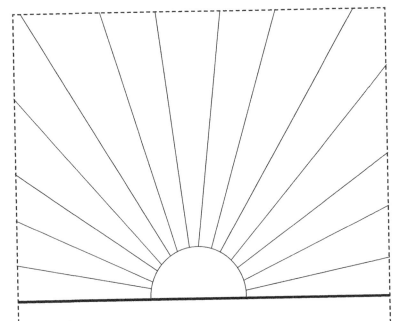

HELLO FROM

SEMINAR IN BRUSSELS

You woud like to go to Brussels for a seminar given by
Donavan Waite sensei. The distance is 150 km and you drive
with an average speed of 110 km per hour. The training starts
at 10 o'clock a.m. Together with Victor, Esmée,
Chris and Rik you will leave from Eindhoven.

▶ At what time will you arrive at the Dojo
in Brussels ?

.... hour

Answer: 150 / 110 = 1 hr and 36 minutes. So the arrival is at 09:36

Ando book   **21**

DOJOS ON EVERY CONTINENT

Aikido is all over the world, on each continent there is an Aikido dojo.

▶ Help Mike write down which continent is which:
Europe / Asia / Africa / Antarctica / Australia
North America / South America

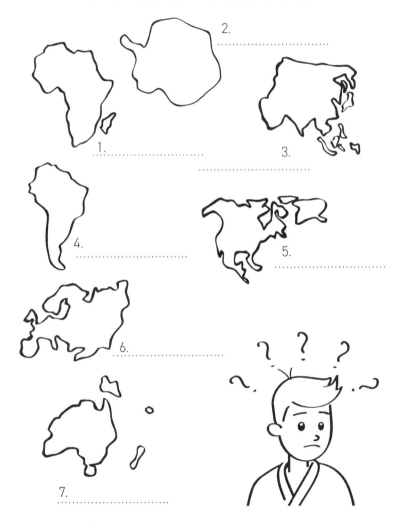

FINISHED EXAMINATION

At Ando dojo it is time for the anual Aikido exams. Sensei made a planning. There will be 15 exams, each one will take 10 minutes and will be conducted by Edo and Anne. The first starts at 10.05 o'clock a.m. and between each there will be a 2 minute break.

▶ At what time will the test be finished? Set the right time by coloring the watch.

Answer: 13:03 (15x 10min + 14 x a break of 2min)

JAPANESE WRITING

Would you like to write your name in Japanese just like Yamada sensei? This is how it is done. In Japan they have a separate alphabet for non-Japanese names. This one is not about how you write your name, but how you PRONOUCE it. So "Penny" will be written like Pe·ni = ペ ニ
Now try it for yourself!

ア a	イ i	ウ u	エ e	オ o	パ pa
カ ka	キ ki	ケ ku	ケ ke	コ ko	ピ pi
サ sa	シ shi	ス su	セ se	ソ so	プ pu
タ ta	チ chi	ツ tsu	テ te	ト to	ペ pe
ナ na	ニ ni	ヌ nu	ネ ne	ノ no	バ ba
ハ ha	ヒ hi	フ fu	ヘ he	ホ ho	ビ bi
マ ma	ミ mi	ム mu	メ me	モ mo	ベ be
ヤ ya	グ gu	ユ yu	ゴ go	ヨ yo	ド do
ラ ra	リ ri	ル ru	レ re	ロ ro	ヂ di
ワ wa	ヰ wyi			ヲ wo	ダ da
ン n	ジ ji				

(The letter L = R in Japanese)

Can your write your own name?
Practice also with other names.

Edo
....

Anne
....

Sam
....

Kim
....

LOST AND FOUND

▶ At the lost and found department we found some items that people forgot after class. Do you know who's stuff it is?

....

....

....

PORTRAIT OF O'SENSEI

▶ Color by number and you'll have
a nice portrait of O'sensei!

0. White
1. Orange
2. Pink
3. Brown
4. Green
5. Yellow

AIKIDO HAIKU

Haiku is a short form of Japanese poetry. Traditionally it's build up like this:

line 1 - 5 syllables
line 2 - 7 syllables
line 3 - 5 syllables

Usually it's about nature or zen, but can you write one about Aikido?

tying your belt
bowling in very slowly
so very boring

ON YOUR WAY TO THE DOJO

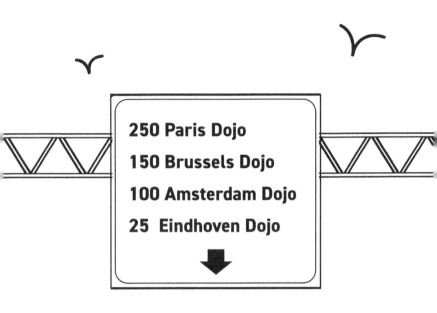

250 Paris Dojo

150 Brussels Dojo

100 Amsterdam Dojo

25 Eindhoven Dojo

▶ How long will it take you to get to the following Dojos? The speed limit is 100 km per hour.

Paris ....

Brussels ....

Amsterdam ....

Eindhoven ....

Answer: P=2,5hr B=1,5hr A=1hr E=15min

28 *Ando book*

THE REAL SAMURAI

▶ Who had the highest score while sensei was drinking his tea? (Add the numbers inside the tire.)

Answer: 664=61 / 994=25 / 649=43 So the samurai is the real samurai!

Ando book **29**

SEMINAR FEE

Sensei Eric takes four of his students out to a seminar. Two of them will train the whole weekend just like him. One of them only trains on Saturday and the other one only on Sunday. With his special teacher's card he is allowed a free seminar, but he forgot the card at home.

Seminar fee

Whole weekend; $50,-
Saturday; $30,-
Sunday; $25,-

▶ Sensei Eric pays at the entrance $250. How much change will he get back? What would the total amount be if he had not forgotten his teacher card?

Answer: $45,- of change / $165,-

ROAN AND THE GEMSTONES

Roan is on his way to his uncle who lives in the woods. He already had his Aikido training and learned a lot from his sensei and sempais. But he has more plans for today because he found some precious stones by the river a few days ago. It is important to know what the value of these stones will be, because they could provide his family and friends with food for a long time. When he arrives at his uncle's house he sees tatami mats on the floor. His uncle sees him while he takes his Obi off. "Good afternoon! What did you bring along? "I found some precious stones a few days ago and hope you can tell me some more about the value". He shows him the stones. "I never saw these before but I'm sure people will pay quite a bit of money for them because they are beautiful and rare". Roan thanks him and leaves in a good spirit. Along the way home he hears a strange noise and suddenly somebody appears right in front of him. It is one of the followers of the enemy Temut. The man is called Kaiden, he remembers him from previous conflicts between their Dojos. Kaiden means fighter, he is well known for his speed, but Roan is not afraid. He has learned how to defend himself in the most dangerous situations. All of a sudden, without any warning, Kaiden draws his Katana and makes a shomen.

Continue the story on page 72, or for a different plot on page 95

BIKING TOGETHER

You are awaiting Lucy to bike together to the dojo. This will take you 10 minutes. It is now 14.00 hrs. 10 minutes ago Lucy texted she is going to be there in 15 minutes.

▶ At what time will you two arrive at the dojo?

A BUSY TRAINING DAY

Stan likes to know what the busiest training day is. Cathy explains that the graph below will tell him. Could you help Stan and point out on which day most of the aikidoka are training?

▶ And what about last season? Was that the same day? How many aikidoka were there on a weekly basis?

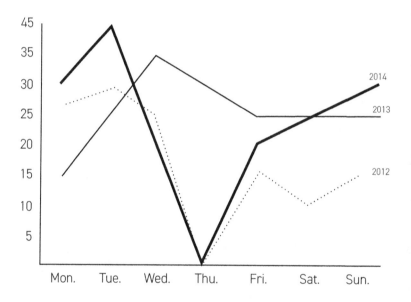

Busiest day: ....

Last season: ....

Number of aikidoka per week: ....

TATAMI FRACTION

Jamie wants to find out how much of the tatami is red.

▶ Can you help him? Simplify the fraction if you can.

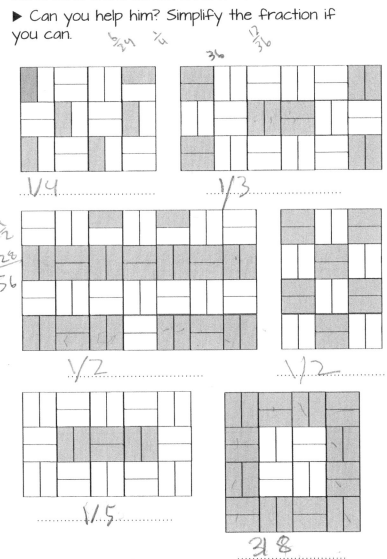

6/24   1/4   12/36   36

1/4   1/3

2/2 28/56

1/2   1/2

1/5

3/8

TATAMI CHAMPION

▶ Do you know who layed the most tatami?
And how many? (Add the numbers on the tatami
and use the paper code to do the math.)

$$2 = 8$$
$$5 = 6$$
$$3 = 9$$

Answer: 23=17 / 33=18 53=15 so the Japanese guy is the champ!

Ando book   **35**

AIRPLANE LUGGAGE

The annual Aikido summer camp, organised by the USAF, is this year in New York. You and a group from Ando will participate at this seminar. You are allowed to take 20 kilos of luggage and 10 kilos of handluggage. You packed the following items:

3 Gi's, each 2600 gram
1 Hakama, 1 kilo
Clothes, total of 5 kilo and 50 gram
Jos and bokkens , total 1950 gram
Swimming gear, total 650 gram
Washing powder, total 100 gram

▶ Is all this not too much, considering the weight you are allowed?

Can you bring back souvenirs?

If so, what will be the maximum weight of the souvenirs?

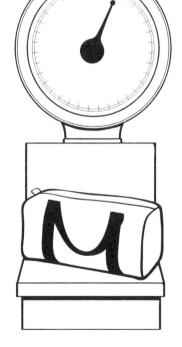

....

....

Answer: Yes / Yes if it's not any more than 8.65 kg
20.000 - (2600 + 1000 + 5050 + 1950 + 650 + 100) = 8650 gram of 8.65 kilo

36   Ando book

THE DRINK MAZE

JAPANESE MATH

A Japanese Kohei asks you to help him with his homework. The sensei has written down some Japanese numbers for you.

▶ Do you think you can help him?

1 = 一		6 = 六	
2 = 二		7 = 七	
3 = 三		8 = 八	
4 = 四		9 = 九	
5 = 五		10 = 十	

二 x 三 = ...

七 + 二 = ...

八 - 一 = ...

六 / 三 = ...

四 + 三 = ...

五 - 二 = ...

四 x 二 = ...

十 / 二 = ...

六 - 五 = ...

八 - 四 = ...

三 x ..... = 九

..... - 六 = 三

四 + ... = 五

九 / ..... = 三

..... + 二 = 十

..... - 三 = 二

七 - ..... = 一

四 x ..... = 八

..... / 二 = 二

九 - ..... = 一

RED TATAMI

▶ How many tatami of 1 square meter can you count in this dojo? How many will you need for a nice red border?

16 meter

40 meter

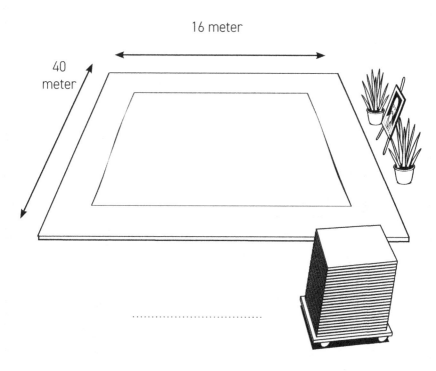

Answer: 640 tatami and 108 for the nice red border.

SAVING MONEY FOR A SEMINAR

You are planning to do a seminar. Can you calculate how long you will have to save money? If you have $122,55 at the bank, $12,45 in your piggy bank. You receive weekly pocketmoney of $1,75 and another $3,25 weekly from your grandmother. For every $10 you save, your parents will give you an extra 5 dollar. You will also receive an extra 50 dollar from your grandmother.

▶ How many months do you have to save money to go to?

$ 260,00 Liege, (Belgium)
$ 380,00 Barcelona, (Spain)
$ 1452,50 New York (USA)

....

....

Answer: On the bank and in the moneypig: $122,55 + $12,45 = $135,00 I save per week: pocketmoney + granny
$1,75 + $3,25 = $5,00
Every two weeks I get from my parents $5 extra because I saved $10,00. So in total I'll have more than $15,00 per two weeks, which is $7,50 per week.
Grandmother pays the last $50,00
The seminar fee is $260,00 - ($50,00 + $135,00) = $75,00
$75,00 / $7,50 = 10 weeks = 2 $\frac{1}{2}$ month
26 weeks or half a year 169 weeks or 3 years and 3 months

JAPANSE MATH TRICK

In Japan they have a clever trick to multiply. Watch the
video on YouTube! For example:

12 x 13

1 ten **2** units **x 1** ten **3** units

Step 1. Put the tens and
units separately, as lines

Step 3. Add the num-
bers at the crossing
of the lines and you
have the answer

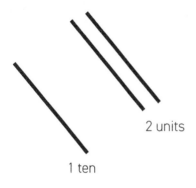

2 units

1 ten

Step 2: Write tens
and units across the
lines in step 1. (13) Tens
on the left, units on
the right

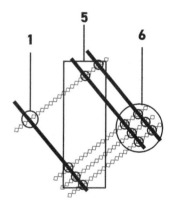

12 x 13 = 156

1 ten

3 units

CALCULATING TATAMIS

Steven is busy organising seminars for coming season. He likes to know how many tatami he has to borrow from their friended Judo dojo. His dojo owns 50 tatami.

▶ How many Aikidoka can tend the seminar? And how many tatami are needed?

2 tatami per Aikidoka

SEMINAR 1
150 Aikidoka

SEMINAR 2
60 Aikidoka

SEMINAR 3
In total we have 118 tatami, how many people can train on it?

WHO WILL TRAIN WITH WHOM

Follow the line and find your training partner.

Elan   Timoer   Robin

Indigo

TATAMI MACHINE

Make a drawing of the tatami laying machine of the future.

COUNTING MEMBERS

Each year Anne and Edo sensei count their members.
In 2011 there were 60 members. In 2012 this grew by 25%. In 2013 they lost 3 members. In the following year they opened a new dojo in Eindhoven which made the number of members 90. The forecast for 2015 is that the total will grow by 10%. 4 members have given notice to stop at the end of the season.

▶ How many aikidoka where member in 2012, 2013, 2014 and what is the prognosis for 2015 ?

2011	2012	2013	2014	2015
60				

Place to take notes:

....

....

....

....

....

....

Answer: 2011=60 members / 2012=75 members (25% x 60 = 15)
60 + 15 = 75 /2013=72 members (75 - 3 = 72) /2014=90 members /
2015=95 members (90 x 10% = 9 - 4 = 5)

SET THE ALARM

Marco can carpool with his sensei to an aikido seminar. The sensei will leave a 7.30hrs. In order not to oversleep Marco must set his alarm, but at what time does he have to get up? Shower and dressing: 20 minutes, packing his bag: 10 minutes. Breakfast, 15 minutes, brushing his teeth, five minutes, spare time: 5 minutes.

▶ At what time does Marco have to set his alarm to be on time? Draw the time on the alarm clock.

Answer: 6:37hr

SPECIAL PANCAKES

This is probably the easiest recipe you ever read before.

Preparation

1. Peel the banana, and crack two eggs in a blender

- 1 banana
- 2 eggs

2. Blend it all together

3. Put a pan on the stove and melt a little butter or use a little oil. Now use the mixture and make the pancake

DOSHU PORTRAIT

During training someone has accidentally put the portrait of Doshu in the wrong order.

▶ Do you know the correct order?

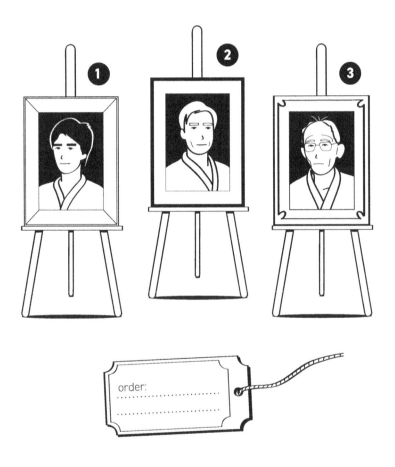

Kisshomaru Ueshiba / Moriteru Ueshiba / Mitsuteru Ueshiba

Answer: 3-2-1

UESHIBA FAMILY TREE

This is a special family portrait, with 3 generations together. All related to Morihei Ueshiba.

▶ Can you complete the family tree of O'sensei?

.... Ueshiba

.... Ueshiba

.... Ueshiba

.... Ueshiba

Ueshiba family

Mitsuteru Ueshiba / Kisshomaru Ueshiba / Moriteru Ueshiba and of course Morihei Ueshiba

Did you know that the son of the Doshu is called "waka sensei"? Waka means "young".

Morihei - Kisshomaru - Moriteru - Mitsuteru

COUPON

Would you like to bring a friend to aikido class? Color the coupon, give it to your friend and he can give it to your sensei when he joins you.

YOUR OWN DOJO

What would you put in your own dojo? Make a drawing.

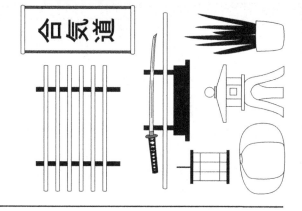

AIKIDO BROWNIE

- 250 gram walnuts
- 325 gram pitted dates
- 125 gram cocoa
- ¼ ts seasalt

Preparation

1. grind the walnuts in a kitchen aid

2. add cocoa, the salt and mix

3. add the dates one by one. The mixture has to be crumbly but also sticky.

4. put the mixture in a baking tin and press it. Leave it in the fridge to cool before you cut it.

PAINTING JAPANESE CHARACTERS

Kirsten is busy painting Aikido characters on the flag.

▶ Can you help her make the flag nicer ?

DARUMA DOLL

A Daruma doll is a Japanese doll and will help you make your wishes come true. When you buy the doll neither one of its eyes are yet painted.

The idea is that you make a wish and color one eye. If your wish comes true you color the other eye.

Did you know people consider the city Takasaki as the place of birth of the Daruma doll? They have a yearly Daruma doll festival.

Tip: You can make your own Daruma doll from a nice rock.

RIGHT FOOT IN FRONT

▶ What is the right footwork for Roys kamae ?

Answer: number four

FOLDING CRANES

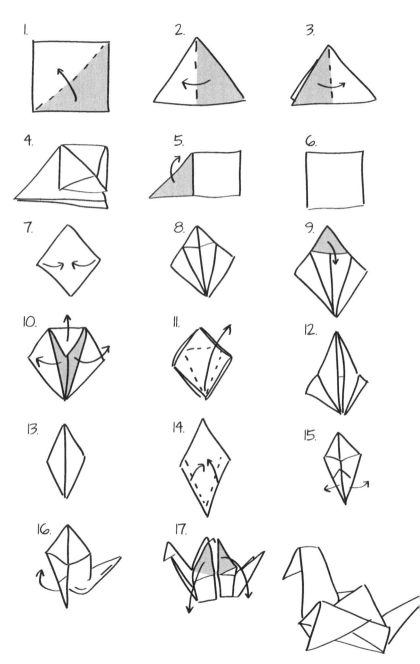

DRAW THE REFLECTION

▶ Do you know the name of this attack?
Finish Victoria's Gi..

....

FOLLOW THE DOTS

If you follow the little dots you can learn how to write Aikido.
Also draw the missing lines till you can write all by yourself.

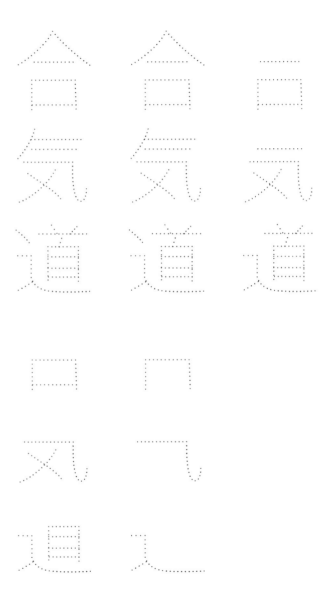

OUCH!

▶ Which technique did John just feel?

S . . . en   U . . .   I . . y .   O m . . .

or was it....

K . t .   D . . i   M . .   . c h .   S . . h . . . g e   U . .

Answer: Shomen Uchi Ikkyo Omote / Kata Dori Men Uchi Shihonage Ura

COLOR THE KIMONO

In the old days people in Japan were dressed in a kimono.
Could you draw a nice design on the kimono?

TECHNIQUES

▶ Do you know which technique is pictured down below? Write the names of the technique underneath the concerning picture.

- ❑ Sokumen iriminage
- ❑ Kokyu ho
- ❑ Tenshi nage

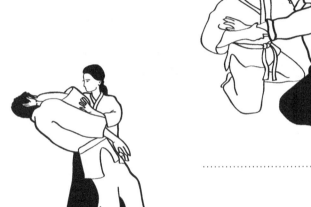

....

....

TECHNIQUES

▶ Do you know which technique is pictured down below? Write the names of the technique underneath the concerning picture.

- ❑ Ikkyo
- ❑ Nikyo
- ❑ Kokyu nage
- ❑ Sankyo
- ❑ Iriminage
- ❑ Shihonage

....

....

....

TECHNIQUES

....

....

....

ATTACKS

▶ Do you know which attack is pictured down below? Write the names of the attack underneath the concerning picture.

- ❏ Shomen uchi
- ❏ Ai hanmi katate dori
- ❏ Katate dori
- ❏ Yokomen uchi
- ❏ Kata dori
- ❏ Mae geri

ATTACKS

▶ Do you know which attack is pictured down below? Write the names of the attack underneath the concerning picture.

❑ Katate ryote dori
❑ Ushiro ryote dori
❑ Chudan tsuki

WORLD TIMES

Ando dojo has taken it upon themselves to organise the world first simultaneous seminar! It will be held in six countries at the same time. In the Netherlands it will start at 10.30 hrs. Japan is 7 hours ahead, Romania is only one hour ahead. New York is six hours earlier, and Brazil three hours. Spain has the same time as the Netherlands and England does not have summertime.

▶ Can you fill in the right times per country?

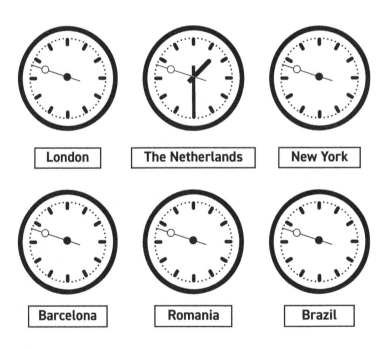

London	The Netherlands	New York

Barcelona	Romania	Brazil

CORRECT KNOT

▶ Mulan has knotted her aikido belt in the dressing-room. Which of the four pictures shows her knot?

Answer: the lowest

BAD ETIQUETTE

▶ What doesn't seem right in this dojo?

Mark the 5 items that are wrong.

Answer: the portrait / bags at the wrong side / zoris near the portrait weapons / no cats on the mat

HAKAMA KNOT

Sam had a hard time putting together his Hakama.

▶ Can you tell which of the four examples is the right one?

Answer: the second one is correct

CHOPSTICKS

Eating with chopsticks is hard in the beginning.. but if you practice every day, like the Japanese, it will soon be easy! Itadakimasu - Enjoy your meal!

Try this: put some M&Ms in a bowl. Use your chopsticks and try to get them from the bowl on your plate (or mouth).

ENDING NO. 1

Roan notices just in time and steps out of the attack line. Only when he notices Kaiden on the floor he realises he has just made a short kaeshi. "Let me go", yells Kaiden. "No", says Roan, "not before you tell me why you attacked me and promise not to attack me again." "I need the gems you have", says Kaiden. "Temu has given me the order to get hold of as many gems as possible to buy some medicine, and not to let anyone stand in my way. Several of our members have fallen ill. Many others have the same order, so please let me go before they find me."

Roan thinks about what Kaiden just said and answers: "I will help you. I'll sell my gems and give you half of the money to buy medicine, but you will have to promise not to attack me again. I know somebody who will buy gems, her name is Umlamuli and she lives in the dark woods." "If you really want to help me, i will not hurt you."

Roan lets go of Kaiden and together they leave to find Umlamuli. Soon they are at her house in the dark woods. On the outside the house looks too small to even make a Mae Kaiten but inside it is so big you could get lost. Umlamuli pays for the gems with golden coins and the medicin Kaiden needs.

After this Roan and Kaiden prepare to leave. Roan tells Kaiden he hopes one day the leaders of the two dojos will realise that together they are stronger. Kaiden agrees and says: "Nothing good will come from this hostility. Thank you for showing me this.".

And with this the two new friends say their goodbyes.

RIGHT FOOT FORWARD

▶ Which footwork belongs to this attack?
Write down the name if you know this.

....

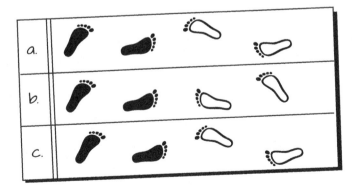

Answer: Katate dori so it's the stand of B

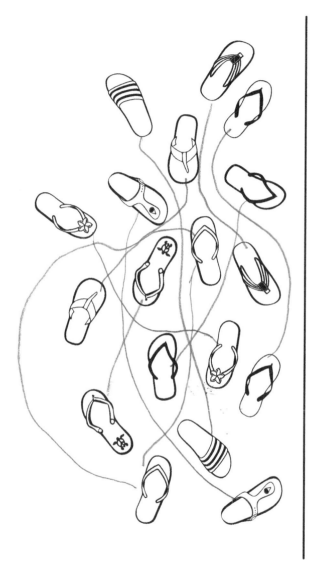

Charlie sensei needs your help. The kids forgot to put their slippers neatly at the end of the mat. Mark the slippers that belong to each other.

SLOPPY TATAMI

Kids placed these tatami very badly...

▶ Do you see where they are badly placed?
Give those tatami a color.

▶ Truth or fiction about tatami?

1. Tatami colours are green/red/blue and yellow	☐ true	☐ false
2. A tatami mat used to be made from straw	☐ true	☐ false
3. Tatami mats of 1x1 meter are better	☐ true	☐ false
4. Tatami mats are often 4 centimeters thick	☐ true	☐ false
5. Red mats are softer	☐ true	☐ false

Answer: 20 tatami's are wrong, 1 true, 2 true, 3 false, 4 true, 5 false

KYU GRADE SIGNS

The wooden signs are not in the correct order.

▶ Can you help Victoria to place them in the right order? Fill out the signs and complete the signs with the kyu grades of your own class.

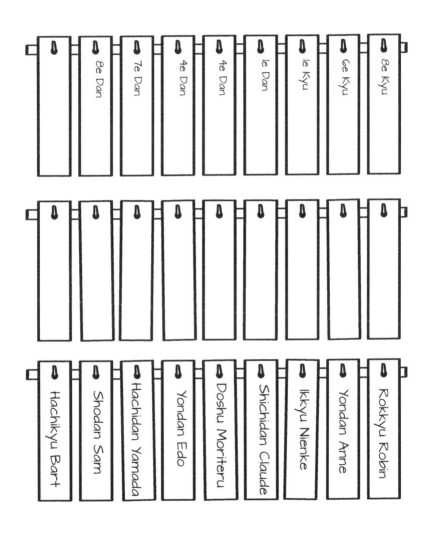

8e Dan · 7e Dan · 4e Dan · 4e Dan · 1e Dan · 1e Kyu · 6e Kyu · 8e Kyu

Hachikyu Bart · Shodan Sam · Hachidan Yamada · Yondan Edo · Doshu Moriteru · Shichidan Claude · Ikkyu Nienke · Yondan Anne · Rokkyu Robin

AIKIDO SCROLLS

▶ Which character of Aikido Ando did Charlie forget to draw? Draw them on the scrolls.

FOLDING YOUR KEIKOGI

The best way to keep you keikogi neat is by folding it
like shown below.

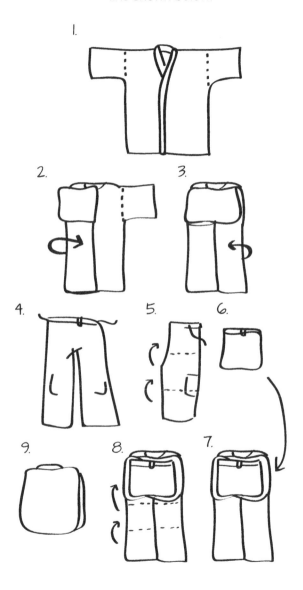

FOLDING THE HAKAMA

The drawings below show you how to fold your sensei's Hakama.

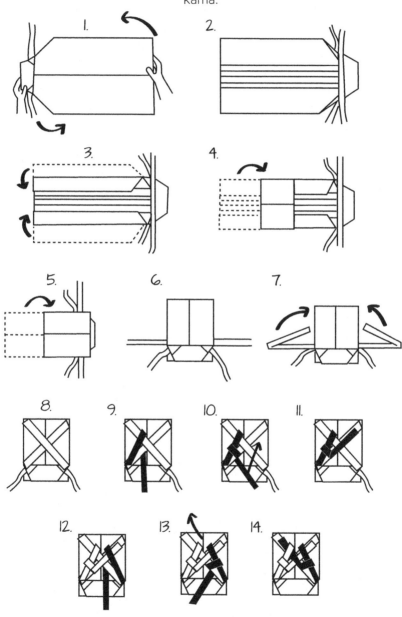

FRESH GI

Never wear a smelly gi again by making a lavender scented sachet to keep your gi fresh in 4 easy steps.

You will need: lavender, scissors, handkerchief, rope

STEP 1.
cut the lavender in little pieces.

STEP 2.
put the lavender in the middle of the handkerchief

STEP 3.
bundle the handkerchief at the top

STEP 4.
Tie the rope around it, and you're done!!

SEMINAR TICKET

Shawn is making the seminar ticket.

▶ Do you know which information should be on the card? Start drawing in the empty ticket below.

Answer: This should be on the ticket, date of the seminar / location / grade of the teacher / entrance fee / time of which part people will practice

Ando book **81**

DOJO AS MEMORY PALACE

How does this work? For example: you want to remember the last names of people. Imagine yourself a palace with many many rooms. In your mind you are walking through the palace and in the bathroom you see a lady taking a shower with water from the creek and using sand as a scrub... Mrs. Sandcreek. Sitting on the toilet you see a man scrubbing his hands with sandpaper... Mr. Sandman. This way Mrs. Thorn can be found in the garden and Mr. Upstairs can be found in the attic. This way you can remember anything you want, not just names! You can even name all the elements in the dojo like in the picture below.

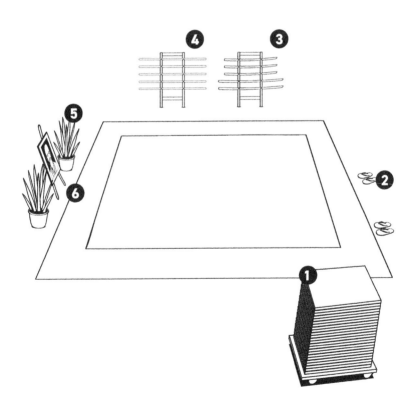

AIKIDOPALS

Draw your best Aikidofriend next to you in the picture below.

FIND THE DIFFERENCES

Answer: Bokken/zori/nose of O'sensei/hairs right/knot of senpai

RICE WITH SATAY

- brown rice (this is much healthier than white rice)
- snap beans, one handful per person
- 1 cucumber
- bean sprouts
- 2-3 eggs
- 3 tablespoons peanut butter
- teaspoon sambal (pepper paste)
- soy sauce
- lemon juice
- milk
- salt

To cook the rice
1. Boil the water. Use one cup of water per one cup of rice.
2. One person needs about half a cup of rice. Add the rice to the water and put in some salt.

Gado Gado
1. Boil the water with the snap beans for about 10 minutes. Add the bean sprouts at the last minute.
2. Boil the eggs until they are hard
3. When cooked put the vegetables in a bowl. Cut some cucumber and mix it with the vegetables.
4. Slice the eggs and lay them on top of the vegetables.

Satay sauce
1. Put 3 tablespoons of peanut butter in a little saucepan. Add 1 teaspoon sambal, some soy sauce, a little bit of lemon juice and milk.
2. Put the saucepan on the stove and keep stirring till the peanut butter melts. Add milk till you have a smooth sauce.

AIKIDO PASSPORT

Horizontal
1. Registration date
2. Person
5. Annual subscription fee
6. Age

Vertical
1. Training
3. Image
4. Ranking

3 Ninja's (1992)

Three young brothers are trained in Ninja technics. They have important powers to fight the badguys. When the brothers are being kidnapped the have to join forces!

Karate Kid (1984)

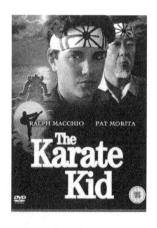

A carpenter/martial arts master decides to teach a boy who's being bullied the art of Karate. He shows him karate is more than just fighting.

"A must see movie"

Kung Fu Panda (2008)

Po the Panda bear is chosen to be the Dragon Warrior in spite of his being overweight and new at the martial arts of Kung Fu.

"One of the best animated movies ever"

BAG MAZE

MAKE YOUR OWN ICE CREAM

Homemade ice cream. Easy, healthy and delicious!

- 200/250 grams of frozen fruit (make your selection in your supermarket)
- 2 tablespoons of honey
- half a glass of yoghurt

Preperation:

1. Put the frozen fruit in a blender (Let your parents take a look while you do this.)

2. Blend as long as you want.. we like little pieces of fruit, so we won't blend too long. (Do this part together with your parents.)

3. Add honey and yoghurt during the blending of the fruit. Don't forget to taste it, so you can decide if you like it sweeter or a little sour.

4. Put everything in the freezer and get it out when it's solid.

READING TIP

Great books to read, or even to do a book review at school.

Children and the Martial Arts: An Aikido Point of View
(Gaku Homma)

Homma sensei uses his personal history, principles, and experience to share so much of what aikido has to offer nowadays.

The Aikido Student Handbook
(Greg O'Connor)

When you just start Aikido this is a great introduction before you enter the dojo to train. It is what it says, a handbook.

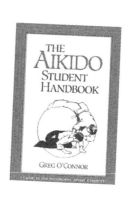

Aikido and the Dynamic Sphere (Adele Westbrook)

One of our own all time favorite. A complete foundation in the practice of one of the most distinctive and effective Japanese martial arts Aikido. Very nice illustrations of all techniques.

CHEAT SHEETS ARE THE BEST WAY TO LEARN

The best way to learn how to summarize is to shorten
everything to one single cheat sheet.

Read a complete
chapter, including
forword and the
concluding remarks.

Write down your
own summary on a
piece of paper, no
more than on one
single sheet.

After this write down
the most important
sentences on a Post-it.

Then make your cheat sheet
with only keywords! Toss it
away before you enter your
class... for sure you know
these words by now!

MAKE A GETA

Make your own traditional Japanese geta just like Nicolas.

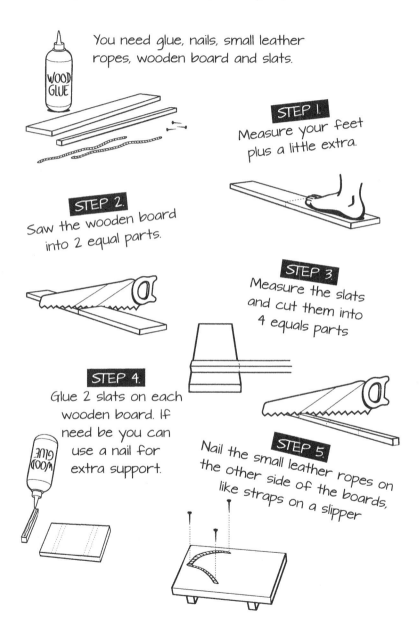

You need glue, nails, small leather ropes, wooden board and slats.

WOOD GLUE

STEP 1.
Measure your feet plus a little extra.

STEP 2.
Saw the wooden board into 2 equal parts.

STEP 3.
Measure the slats and cut them into 4 equals parts

STEP 4.
Glue 2 slats on each wooden board. If need be you can use a nail for extra support.

STEP 5.
Nail the small leather ropes on the other side of the boards, like straps on a slipper

THIS WATER TASTES BETTER

Anne has some tips to spice up your water!

▶ Add some lemon, cucumber
or fresh mint to your water.

COMMUNICATING

ENDING NO. 2

Roan notices it just in time, steps out of the line of attact and runs! He zigzags between the trees and stumbles over a treelog. His first instinct is of course mae kaiten so he's up again in a second.

After six minutes Roan rests, believing he has shaken him off. But he has not seen Temut followers ,they surround him now. Roan also sees that Kaiden has a tanto, and others also carry weapons. There are more tantos and he also sees a jo. Roan knows how to defend himself against these weapons but he needs to be cautious and focus. "Give us your gems", one of his followers yells. "No way", Roan answers, "we need them ourselves. You'll have to find your own way to acquire valuables in an honest way."

The followers answer with attack such as tsuki, yokomen uchi and katate dori..

Roan defends with shiho nage, tenchi nage and kokyu ho and manages to take Kaidens katana which ends the attack. "But we really need your gems", says one of the followers, but Roan runs. He doesn't want them to know he is not trained enough with bokkens or a katana.

Kaiden and the others do not follow him. Back in his village Roan tells his sensei what has happened. His sensei warns him not to wander in the woods and tells him he will find out why the others have wandered so far from their dojo. This calms Roan and it makes him feel safe knowing his sensei will keep an eye out for him. Reassured after this unexpected and for now still unexplained adventure, Roan returns home.

HIGHT TATAMI PILE

▶ Brian piles the tatami mats high up! Do you think that's ok? How many mats does Brian have to take down?

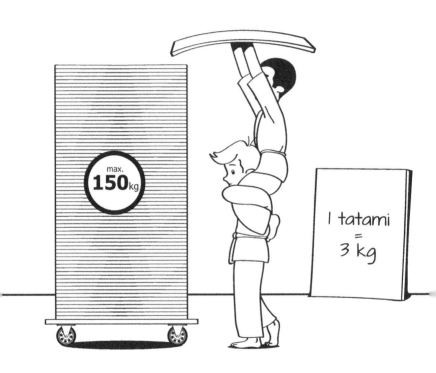

AIKIDO JUMPING—JACK DOLL

Cut out the doll, connect the rope like in the picture on little pins and you have your own jumping-jack doll.

SUGAR SWEET

Water
0 Gram
CH

Sports drink
70 Gram
CH

Cola
35 Gram
CH

▶ Write down per item how many sugar cubes they contain.

....

Answer: coke: 7 / sportsdrink 14 / water none

TATAMI OUTLINE

▶ What is the outline of the mats below?

mat 1.
....

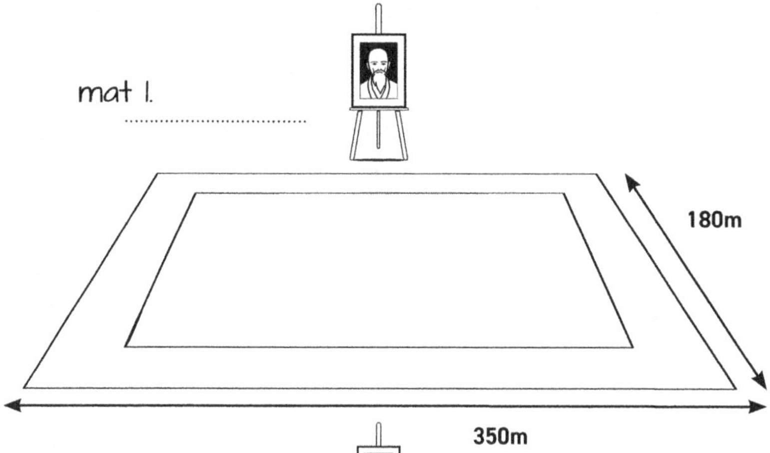

180m

350m

mat 2.
....

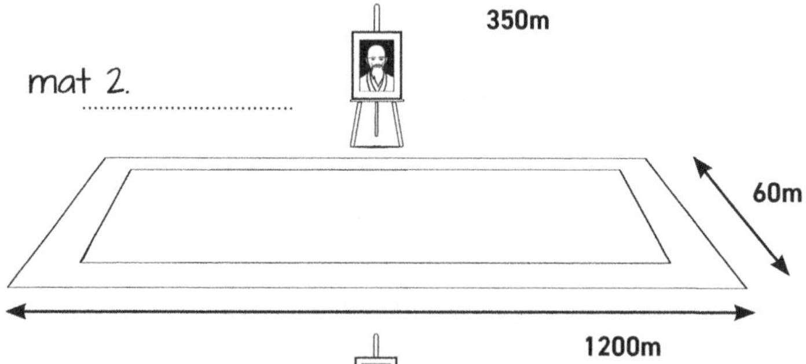

60m

1200m

mat 3.
....

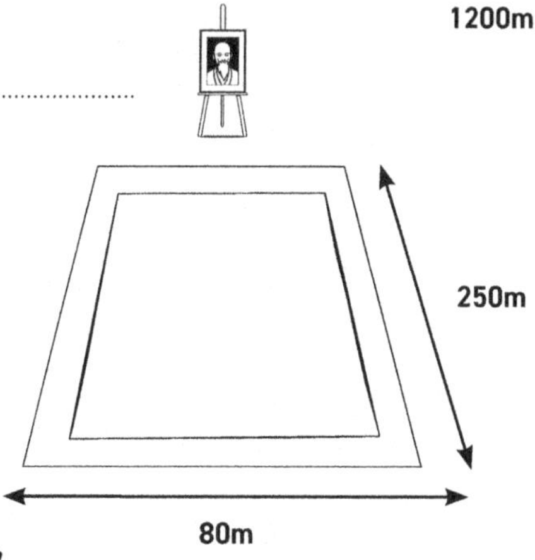

250m

80m

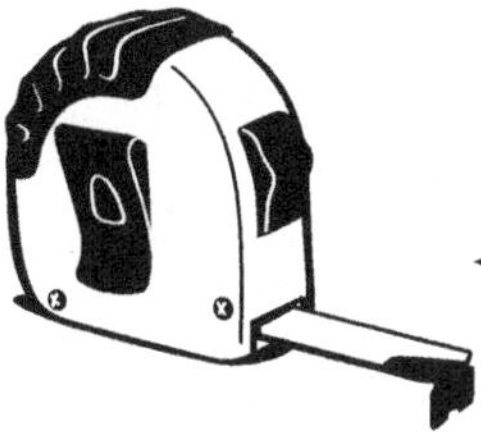

Answer: 1=1,060m 2=2,520m 3=660m

FIRST AID IN THE DOJO

Aikido is not a sport with a lot of injuries. But your sensei will recommend to have your own First aid kit for minor injuries. Crucial for big seminars.

In your kit you should have

- a sling
- tweezers
- gauze 5x5 cm
- bottle of lavender oil
- dextrose
- band aid
- scissors
- sterilized gauze
- sporttape
- elastics
- pair of nail clippers

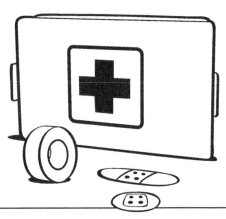

Did you know that when you put a few drops of laveder oil on a scratch it will take the pain away? Well now you do! People with diabetes can feel a bit weak during the training, usually some dextrose will help instantly.

KNOW YOUR WAY IN FRENCH

1 **Je m'appelle .... Je suis Anglaise et J'habite en ....**
I am (fill out your name) and I am English
I am from (fill out the place you live)

2 **Où sont les toilettes s'il vous plait?**
Where is the toilet ?

3 **Je cherche le Dojo d'aïkido**
I am looking for a dojo, do you know where I can find one?

4 **Je voudrais payer le stage, c'est combien?**
I would like to pay for the seminar do you know how much it is?

5 **Les vestiaires pour les femmes/hommes, s'il vous plait?**
Where is the dressing room for men/women ?

10 Mots importants

Hello	-	Salut/ Bonjour
Straight on	-	Tout droit
Left	-	Gauche
Right	-	Droite
Information desk	-	Bureau d'information
Register	-	Registre
Entrance ticket	-	Ticket (d'entrée)
Cafeteria	-	Cantine
Thanks	-	Merci
Goodbye	-	Au revoir

AIKIDO MAKES THE SENTENCE

Before I enter .... I greet the .... that is
the site where the portrait of .... is. I get changed and
put my .... on and put my .... at the edge of
.... Today is weapon class, that means that we all have
our .... and .... with us but also our .... ,
because you do not know what the .... will choose to
train with. In this training only .... needs his weapon to
attack. This technique is Ikkyo, this is a technique without making an .... Because it is not possible to do ura, we will do
.... first. Bart is higher in rank so as a .... he starts
with the technique. After a few attempts we swapped and when
.... saw us, he explained to me how it was done. While he
showed me I had to take place in .... Before I knew this
class was already over. At the end we all said at the same time
................., that means thank you for this class.

WHAT IS WHAT

▶ Do you think you know all these words without using an Aikido book or the internet? If not you may ask your sempai for help.

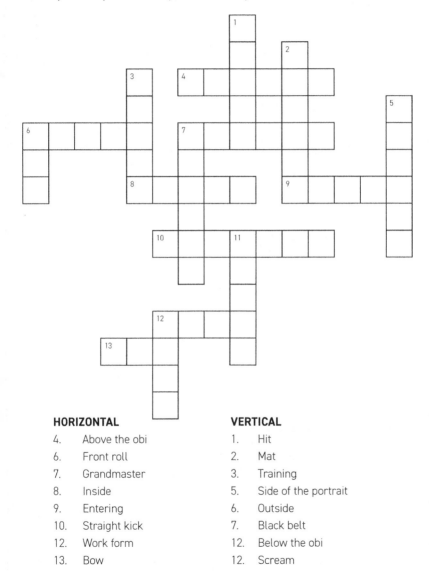

HORIZONTAL

4. Above the obi
6. Front roll
7. Grandmaster
8. Inside
9. Entering
10. Straight kick
12. Work form
13. Bow

VERTICAL

1. Hit
2. Mat
3. Training
5. Side of the portrait
6. Outside
7. Black belt
12. Below the obi
12. Scream

WHICH ATTACK IS WHERE

Focus and draw a line to places were
you attack.

0 Jodan tsuki

0 Chudan tsuki

0 Shomen Uchi

0 Yokomen uchi

0 Kata dori

0 Mae geri

THE HAKAMA CREASES

Did you know that a hakama has 7 creases? 5 are on the front and 2 at the back. They all have a meaning. Connect them, you may look it up on the internet.

JIN   o   o   Politeness
GI   o   o   Honesty
REI   o   o   Help one another
CHI   o   o   Dedication
SHIN o   o   Be nice

CHU   o   o   Wisdom
KOH   o   o   Honour and justice

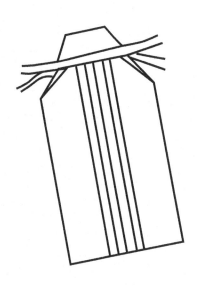

Answer: 1=5 2=7 3=1 4=6 5=2 6=3 7=4

ETIQUETTE

▶ Do you know what is not allowed on the tatami? And can you find the other words in the puzzle?

s	c	r	a	t	c	h	i	n	g
d	e	a	k	m	i	x	v	h	h
i	n	x	x	s	g	m	u	s	s
r	o	v	r	o	k	s	g	d	t
t	h	d	d	b	k	n	m	n	r
y	p	o	w	b	i	j	i	t	a
g	x	o	z	r	t	t	x	r	w
i	h	f	r	m	r	o	i	b	d
b	n	a	h	r	a	i	g	n	p
n	e	o	x	h	f	w	f	c	g

earrings
food
drinks
phone
scratching
biting
dirty gi
chewing gum
warts
fart

A	S	O	X	J	N	A	F	S	U	I
K	T	O	R	I	O	B	H	A	M	M
C	D	H	T	A	N	T	O	M	Z	N
Y	O	A	B	E	I	U	B	U	K	A
R	S	K	O	Z	G	N	V	R	W	H
V	H	A	K	I	O	A	T	A	E	B
D	U	M	K	E	K	D	N	I	K	R
H	O	A	E	S	I	O	I	R	V	H
E	H	J	N	N	E	H	H	K	V	Q
V	K	S	O	E	K	S	R	X	I	E
V	Q	U	F	S	N	L	J	E	Y	A

samurai
keikogi
aikido
jo
tanto
bokken
sensei
shodan
hakama
uke
tori
nage
hanmi
doshu
dojo

KNOW YOUR WAY IN SPANISH

① **Me llamo .... Soy Inglés, Vivo en ....**
I am (fill out your name),
II am from (fill out your home town)

② **Los aseos por favor?**
Where is the toilet?

③ **Sabe dónde está el dojo de aikido**
I am looking for a dojo , do you know where I can find one?

④ **Cuánto cuesta el curso?**
I would like to pay, how much is the seminar?

⑤ **Los vestuarios para mujeres/hombres por favor?**
Where is the dressing room for the men / women?

10 Palabras importantes

Hello /Hi	-	Hola
Straight on	-	Todo recto
Left	-	Izquierda
Right	-	Derecha
Information desk	-	Mostrador de información
To register	-	Inscripción
Entrance ticket	-	Tarjeta de entrada
Cafeteria	-	Cantina
Thank you	-	Gracias
Good bye	-	Adiós

WHAT TYPE OF SENSEI ARE YOU

Which answer matches you?
Circle them and add the numbers.

Do yo like a long warming up?
3: Not too long but breathing exercises are important
1: Yes it is nice to stretch and relax
4: No. Warming up the primar muscles is my priority
2: Yes warming up is the basic

Which techniques you like most?
3: grips
1: Randori
2: throwing
4: Basic technics

Do you like to train with weapons?
4: Not more than other do
2: Yes that is an important aspect of Aikido
3: No but is is important
1: Yes i like tanto during class training

What language do you like?
4: Japanese
1: Spanish
3: English
2: French

Who is your favourite?
2: Kanai sensei
1: Yamada sensei
4: Kisshomaru sensei
3: Tohei sensei

Doshu Moriteru   **12-20**

I train a lot with large Aikido groups (1.000+) so I stick to the basics so it is clear for everybody. And I can speak Japanese because there is always a translator.

Yoshimitsu Yamada   **9-12**

I start most of the time earlier so I can do my own warming up. I enjoy a lot a technique like Nikyo, but i only use weapons to make a statement. My favourite language is English because I live in the U.S.A. But I can speak Japanese.

Claude Berthiaume   **6-9**

If you are in good shape you can train longer. Especially if you are tossed around (like my teacher Kanai does) After the training I practice with a real katana. In the dojo I speak French but I also speak English.

Michelle Feilen   **3-6**

Flexibility is very important, especially if you want to practice randori. I like to train with the tanto, even if my teacher Yamada sensei does not use it often. My native language is Spanish.

AIKI—BINGO!!

Cut out the tickets and watch some Aikido demonstration clips on Youtube. And see who wins the bingo!

ビンゴ bingo ビンゴ

SHOMEN UCHI	IRIMINAGE	USHIRO RYOTE DORI
KOTE GAESHI	TSUKI	JO DORI
KOKYU NAGE	MAE GERI	SANKYO

ビンゴ bingo ビンゴ

IKKYO	SHIHONAGE	KOSHINAGE
TSUKI	TENCHI NAGE	YOKOMEN UCHI
KATADORI	RANDORI	TANTO

MEDITATION PAGE

Think as a tree, you are rooted firmly in the ground. Your leaves breathe... The sunlight will give you energy to grow. Breathe in and out. Isn't it nice to be such a beautiful strong tree?

TANGRAM

Cut out all the figurines and put them in the right order.

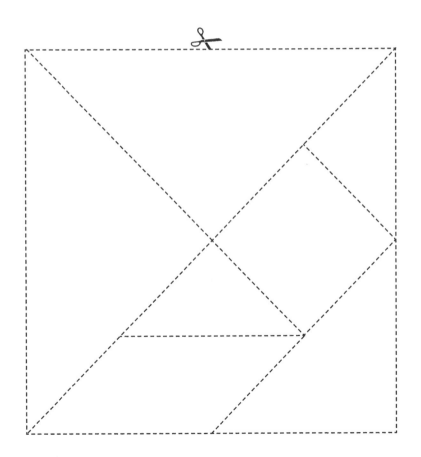

LET'S PLAY DICE

Cut out this dice and practise on the tatami.

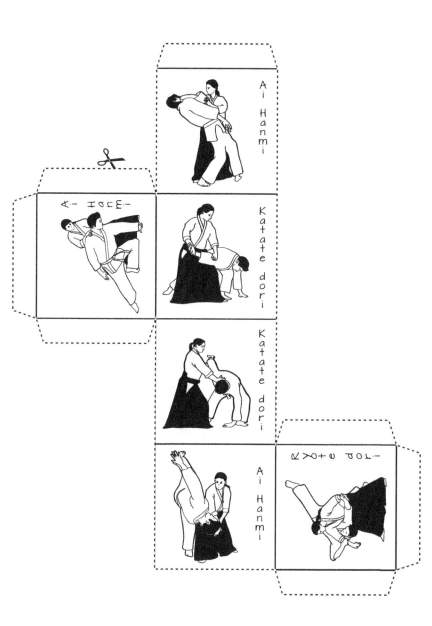

INGREDIENTS

▶ Do you know which ingredients you see on this plate? Can you classify them?

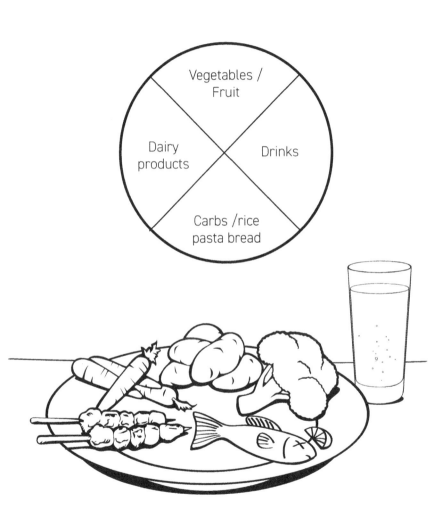

Vegetables / Fruit

Dairy products

Drinks

Carbs /rice pasta bread

Answer: Fish, meat (on the stick), cauliflower, patatoes, carrots

AIKIDO QUARTET

Shuffle the cards and hand them out. The winner has
4 matching cards.

GROW YOUR OWN

It is so much fun to have your own vegetable garden. From the tiny seed to that first bite in your own grown tomato. Picture this? You only need some soil, seeds and markers in the ground so you know what you planted. Of course do not forget to water the plants

All you need are seeds!

AURA COLOURING PICTURE

Your aura is the energy space around you. Some people can actually see it or make a picture. All the colours have a meaning like we wrote down underneath. Colour Michelle's aura.

Red: determined
Orange: caring
Yellow: creative
Green: compassive
Blue: adventurous
Indigo: responsible
Violet: spiritual
Silver: sensitive
Gold: successful
Pink: loving
White: pure

AIKIDO FRIENDS PAGES

Ask your friends to write something about you.

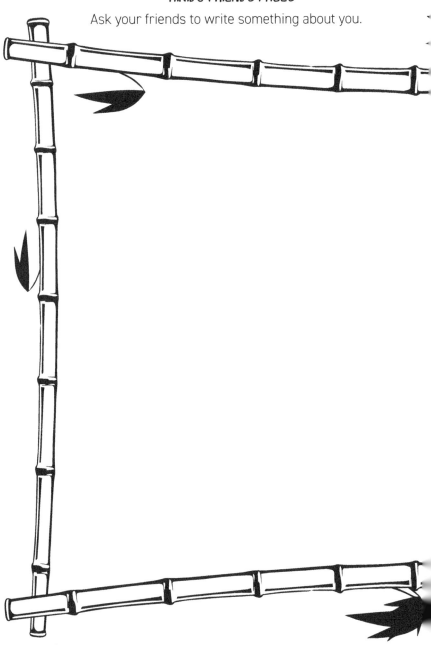

MANDALA COLOURING PICTURE

Originally a Mandala was made of coloured sand. It took monks weeks to make one. You can use a colored pen.

NICE CUP OF TEA

Besides the fact that tea is tasty, it can also have different effects on you. Chamomille tea is a good remedy for a sore throat. Check out these 3 Japanese teas.

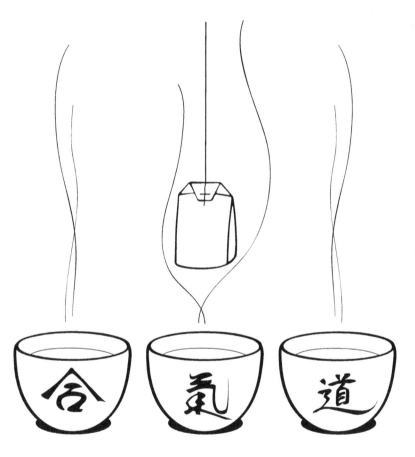

Green tea
Used to be a medication because it is good for your health.

White tea
Also good for your health and helps you loose weight.

Black tea
This tea has an intense flavour.

LEFT AND RIGHT

....

....

....

....

....

....

Write above the obi: I love Aikido with your right hand

and below with your left hand.

....

....

....

....

....

....

THE DRESSING ROOM

What is wrong in this dressing room?
Circle your answers.

MAKING ICE TEA

Preparation

1. Boil some water and add the teabags for about 4 minutes. The longer you will the teabag the stronger the tea.

2. Cut a piece of fresh ginger and put it in the warm tea.

3. Stir some honey, the more the sweeter

4. Add some slices of lemon and let it all cool down in the fridge.

5. Serve it cold with some extra ice cubes if you like and leave the lemon and ginger.

- 1 liter of water
- 2 or 3 bags of mint tea
- piece of ginger
- slice of lemon
- 1. spoon of honey

CALCULATOR TRICK

All you need is a calculator. When you hold it in your hand say some magic words. Now it has that magic spell and can reveal some secrets.

You will ask your magic machine some questions, it will calculate the age and house number of your friend.

You ask him to insert the following data.

> Enter your house number
> Double that number
> Plus 42
> Multiply that figure with 50
> Deduct your year of birth
> Deduct another 50
> Did you add your birthday of this year already?
> Yes= plus 1 or no= plus zero. Deduct 37

Now I am telling you that the first two numbers is your age and the other is your house number. Make the trick in 2015, and deduct at the end 36 instead of 37.

THE KATANA MAZE

AIKIDO KARAOKE

▶ Martin Solveig - Hello (Aikido lyrics)

I can't stick around and talk with you, noo ohohhh
It doesn't really mean that I don't like you, nooo ohohh

I like talking to though but I came to aikido now
But don't take it the wrong way cause that's all you get from me, hey

Yeah I think it's nice, but I really think that you should know
I just came to aikido, aikido, aikido, aikido oh oh ohh

I'm not the kinda girl to mess around with now, noo ohhohh
I'm let you try just attack me now, shomen ohohohh

It's alright I like the training just keep aikidoing
It's OK with me if you don't have that much to say, hey

Yeah I like the sensei but there's something you should know
I just came to aikido, aikido, aikido, aikido ohohoohh

I can't stick around and talk with you, noo ohohh
It doesn't really mean that I don't like you, nooo ohohh

I like talking to though but I came to aikido now - 7x
I just came to aikido, aikido, aikido, aikido ohohhh

I'm not the kinda girl to mess around with now, noo ohhohh
I'm let you try just attack me now, shomen ohohohh

It's alright I like the training just keep aikidoing
It's OK with me if you don't have that much to say, hey

Yeah I like the sensei but there's something you should know
I just came to aikido, aikido, aikido, aikido ohohoohh

MAGIC CARD TRICK

Let a drinking glass hover on a playing card. All you need is playing cards and double sided adhesive tape and some time to practice.

❶

Get your playing cards and find the joker. Fold it and tape it to another card.

Make sure nobody sees the backside.

❷

To make people choose the magic card you will hold it on the bottom of the pile. You will shuffle them till he says STOP and then you get the special card and perform the trick.

DRAW YOUR DOJO IN TO THIS LANDSCAPE

MAKE YOUR OWN CROSS-BOW

You'll need: 2 wooden sticks, a cap, elastic, skewer and a pin.

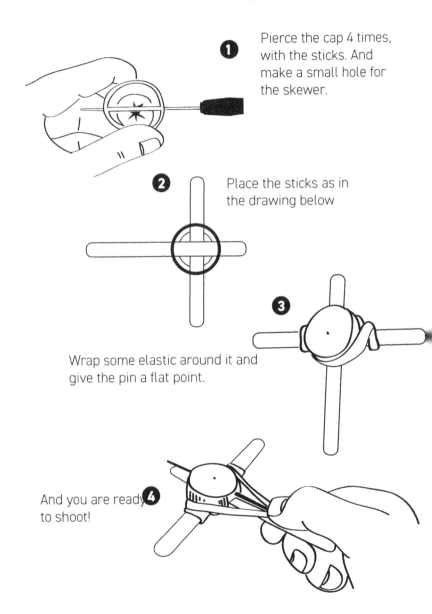

1 Pierce the cap 4 times, with the sticks. And make a small hole for the skewer.

2 Place the sticks as in the drawing below

3 Wrap some elastic around it and give the pin a flat point.

4 And you are ready to shoot!

KNOW YOUR WAY IN JAPANESE

1 **Watashi wa .... Eigo wo hanashimasu,**
Watashi wa .... shusshindesu
I am (fill in your name) I speak English,
I am from (fill in place)

2 **Benjo wa doko desu ka?**
Where is the toilet?

3 **Watashi wa Aikido dōjō o sagashiteimasu**
I am looking for an Aikido dojo

4 **Watashi ga shiharau no ga suki. Seminā wa ikuradesu ka?**
I would like to pay. How much is the seminar?

5 **Koko de dansei no gakuyadesu /**
Doko de josei no kōi-shitsudesu
Where is the male / female dressingroom?

安
道

10 important words

konnichiwa	-	Hello
masugu	-	Straight (ahead)
hidari	-	Left
migi	-	Right
An'naisho	-	Information desk
Tōroku	-	Register
Nyūjō-ken	-	Ticket
Resutoran	-	Restaurant
arigatōu	-	Thank you
sayōunara	-	Bye

MAKE A JAPANESE LANTERN

You need: some paper, glue and a pair of scissors.

1 Cut of a small piece of paper for the handle.

2 Fold the paper in two and cut little strokes of 1,5cm (stop before you cut the paper off completely).

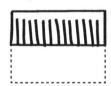

3 Open up the paper.

4 Fold the paper around and glue it together. Finish off with the handle of the lantern.

Tip: When you take the size of a drinking glass, you can keep the glass inside and use it as a candle holder.

WRITE YOUR OWN AIKIDO STORY

One upon a time there was an Aikidoka always early home from school. But not today... He had to help his teacher cleaning up. That's why it was already dark when he picked up his bicycle. He was not afraid in the dark but there was always a small crowd in the bike shelter. And they were there today as well............

....

....

....

....

....

....

....

....

....

....

....

....

....

....

DYNAMIC READING

Get your book and choose a full page. Pick a word in the middle of the page and focus on it. While focusing think about how many other words you can see without moving your eyes? So keep staring at the one word you choose.

And? How many words did you see? Most of the people will see between 3 to 8 words. Our eyes can pick up the information much faster then we think. Speedreaders read groups of words at once. That's what you just experienced. It is important to know many words. So if you read a word you do not know, find the meaning. On page 138 you will find a story. Please try to read with your eyes in the middle of the story. You will see a thin line in the text. Try to read all the words without moving the eyes. It's a great exercise.

THIS IS HOW YOU RELAX

It is Wednesday morning, nobody talks to you. Too bad.
You feel alone. How will I make my test later on? You are not
sure you learned enough. You stop breathing for a moment.
You are a bit in a panic. "Relax", you hear a little voice in your
head. Don't be afraid. Take a deep breath and empty your lungs.
3 times. You will feel more comfortable. It feels nice when the
stress is gone. Your breath is your best friend. You can have
mini breaks whenever you like during the day. Just focus on
your breathing. Be aware of your breathing.

Look at the clock and put one hand on your belly.
Breath in through your nose and out through
your mouth. Feel your belly rise up and down. Do
this for one minute, it's ok if your mind wanders
off, Just bring back your attention to the clock
again and focus for one minute. You can do that!

Ando book **137**

HOW TO SCAN

Try not to read the text but scan it. This may take some time but that's ok. Follow the line, this will make it easier.

To breath,
to walk To eat
To drink, To take a leak,
to defecate,
To dream, to dance, to enjoy,
to play football, to calculate,
to think about...
All these matters are in your head.
That is where your brains are
And they work for you day and night

Without you having to think about it
The brains consist of billions of nerve cells
About a 100 billion
And every one is connected to another 1000
to 10.000 other cells
It is like a very complicated spider web.
They constantly comunicate to another
by sending information to each other.
For example from head to toe and
back again.

YOUR OWN ZEN GARDEN

A Japanese garden (karesansui), or Zen garden is a shallow tank with sand, pebbles and some grass or other elements of nature. You can use sand to create the effect of water and make patterns. Being busy in the garden is relaxing and brings peace and harmony.

This is how to make one!

Buy some fine sand and make a nice wooden box or use an old wooden tray from your mother. Put the sand on it and make a nice pattern with some pebbles or make lines in the sand. You can use an old hairbrush as a rake. Glue some nice little rocks together and put them in the corners.
You can always alter your garden.That is all up to you.
Do some breathing exercises and enjoy your Zen garden.

IRON WRITING

It is very simple, use milk as ink! You can make a nice drawing or do some secret writing. All you have to do is iron the piece of paper to see what you wrote down. Let's give it a try!

You'll need: Milk and an empty fountain pen or a little brush. Paper and an iron.

Write your message and then iron it when it's dry.

ARE YOU ALERT ?

You have been reading a lot of pages already but how focused were you ?Do yo know the answers to the following questions ?

1. How do you say in French : Where can I find the toilet?

....

2. What is the content of the karaoke song?

....

3. How did the monks make a Mandala?

....

4. What does the 'Jin' crease mean?

....

5. Were the boy and girl talking about the same dog?

....

6. What do you need to make your own ice cream?

....

7. How can you easy remember things?

....

8. What can you do with the Daruma doll ?

....

Answers can be found on page 131/127/120/105/94/89/82/54

NO JO? THIS IS HOW YOU MAKE ONE!

Talk to your parents first before you make your Jo.
Tip: Don't use a very heavy broom stick.

You need: broom, saw and some sandpaper

STEP 1
Cut off the end of the broom,
so you have only the stick.:

STEP 2
Measure it to fit
under your armpit

STEP 3.
Adjust the size and make
both sides nice and
smooth with sandpaper.
And there is your Jo!

MIKA—JO

▶ Chris is in bed with glowing Mikado sticks. Can you see whose Jo is at the bottom?

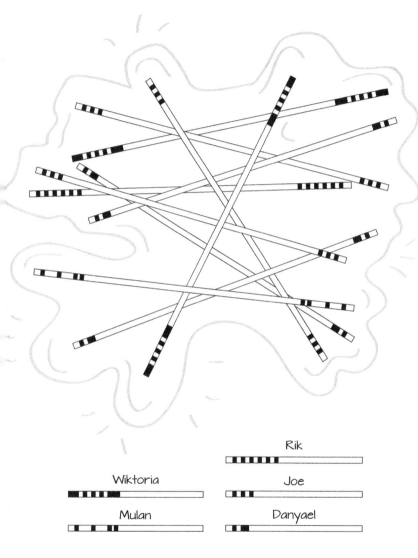

Rik

Wiktoria

Joe

Mulan

Danyael

Answer: Danyael

FOLD YOUR OWN PAPER FOX

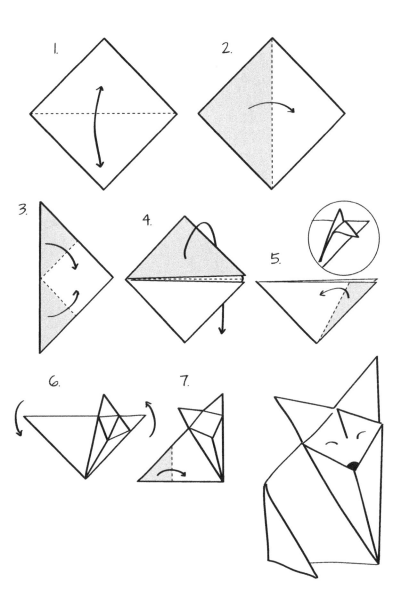

1.

2.

3.

4.

5.

6.

7.

A LOT OF RICE

That Asian people eat a lot of rice may not be so shocking. But did you realize there are a lot of products with rice?

▶ **Name as many products you know that contain rice.**

....

....

....

....

....

....

....

Answer: Rice pudding, rice candy, rice crackers, rice cake, sake (wine) rice soup, sushi

HOW TO DRAW A PANDA

*that is not
a nice panda*

You don't have to be an artist to make a <u>nice panda</u>.
Let's give it a try !

1.

4.

2.

5.

3.

6.

MAKE A DRAWING OF A PANDA IN A NICE BASKET

DRAW AND CUT YOUR OWN AIKIDO PUZZLE

RICE LEFT OVERS

- rice
- butter
- sugar
- cinamon

Preparation

1. Reheat some rice in the microwave or oven.

2. Add some butter and cane sugar.

3. And some cinnamon to finish it.

MAP READING

▶ Do you know where these streets are on the map?

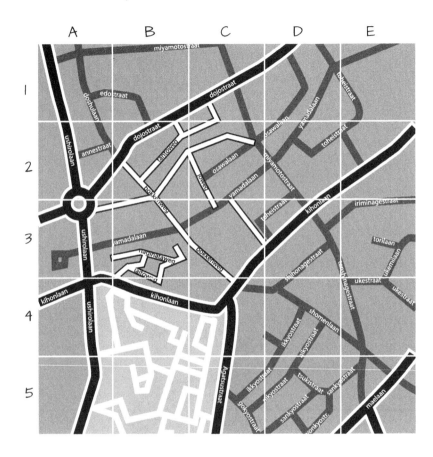

Ikkyostraat	5C + 5D	Torilaan	....
Osawalaan	....	Kihonlaan	....
Gokyostraat	....	Toheistraat	....
Yamadalaan	....	Joweg	....
Tsukistraat	....	Iaitoweg	....

THE BONSAI

Bonsai is Japanese, and means tree in a pot. The First bonsai trees came from nature and were placed to improve the
courtyards at monasteries. Taoïsts adored nature and nature in
its perfection. The tree in the pot was perfect and did not need
a lot of trimming.The Japanese were the masters of trimming.
New techniques were found and the trees were simplified. Just
like the Japanese gardens the bonsai trees reflected a mini nature. Rich people showed their favourite tree in their teahouse.
And so it became a symbol of status.

STAY COOL

Cut out and fold on the line and you made your own little fan.

THE PANDA MAZE

KEEP UP THE SPIRIT

▶ How do you feel during the week? Is there a difference in the weeks when you went to Aikido training?

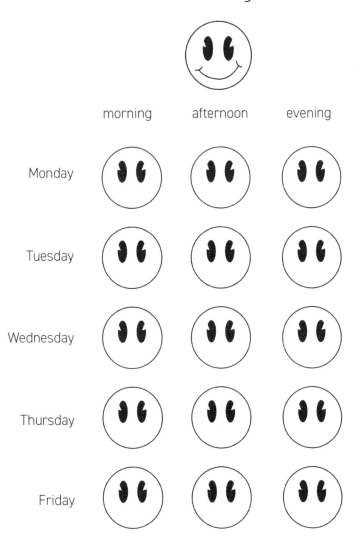

Made in the USA
Coppell, TX
03 April 2020